A Very Little Office of
Compline

Night Prayer for Children

Compiled and Adapted by
B.G. 'Odo' Bonner, Obl. O.S.B.

Illustrated by
Gwyneth Thompson-Briggs

TAN Books
Gastonia, North Carolina

A Very Little Office of Compline: Night Prayer for Children © 2025 Bo Bonner

All rights reserved. With the exception of short excerpts used in critical review, no part of this work may be reproduced, transmitted, or stored in any form whatsoever, without the prior written permission of the publisher. Creation, exploitation and distribution of any unauthorized editions of this work, in any format in existence now or in the future—including but not limited to text, audio, and video—is prohibited without the prior written permission of the publisher.

The original prayers were taken from the Latin-English Monastic Diurnal, 8th Edition from St. Michael's Abbey, and the Latin-English pamphlets for all 8 offices from Abbey Editions, the imprint of Clear Creek Abbey. All rhymes are original, although of course heavily influenced through repeated prayer of the English translations noted above.

Illustrated by Gwyneth Thompson-Briggs

Cover design by Jordan Avery

ISBN: 978-1-5051-3506-0
Kindle ISBN: 978-1-5051-3659-3
ePUB ISBN: 978-1-5051-3657-9

Published in the United States by
TAN Books
PO Box 269
Gastonia, NC 28053

www.TANBooks.com

Printed in India

A Very Little Office of
Compline

Night Prayer for Children

The Very Little Hours

Matins speaks from silence deep
as Lauds, the dawning harvests reap

Prime, our labors, girds with strength
as Terce prepares our votive's length

Sext bears the Cross on which Christ hung
'til "it is finished" by None be sung

Then Vespers lights the lamps of praise
and Compline rests our pilgrim days

Seven-a-Day I bow my chin
and once at night to conquer sin.
Amen.

A Very Little Compline

Incipit

May the almighty God grant me a blessing
and a quiet night peaceful for resting
and when life brings me to my final day
may the Lord perfect it in every way.
Amen.

Lectio Brevis

May our passions be never inflamed
nor our souls by the devil be maimed
who like a lion may roar
while we slumber and snore
but our help's in the name of the Lord!

Confiteor

May God grant mercy,
forgive us our sin
and bring us to Heaven
where life never ends

May He grant us His pardon
absolve and remit,
and we, to His loving
embrace readmit.
Amen.

Psalm 4

When I called upon my just God, lo
He turned His ear to me

When I shrank from tribulation
He magnified and set me free

In peace like a verdant harvest
I will sleep and take my rest

The Lord has settled me uniquely
in a hope that is the best.
Amen.

Psalm 90

Like a shield Your truth protects me
from the terrors of the night

A thousand may fall beside me
but to me it comes not nigh

You have given in charge of me
Your Angels along my way

No stone to dash my foot on
as it tramples the beasts that lay.
Amen.

Psalm 133

Behold now bless the Lord, ye
who stand in the house of God

Lift your hands to the holy places
bless He Who made sky and sod.
Amen.

Hymn

Before the day is done
Creator of earth and sun
Your favor please endow
both guard and keep us now

From nightmares and their fear
defend mind, eye, and ear
tread underfoot the fiend
and keep our conscience clean

To the Father and the Son,
and the Spirit, Three-in-One
be all glory now and ever
Who live and reign forever!
Amen.

Little Chapter and Verse

Chapter

But Lord, You are among us
and Your name is invoked upon us
may Your love never forsake us
Our Lord and God above us.

Thanks be to God.

Verse

Into Your hands, O Lord, into Your hands, O Lord
into Your hands, my spirit, I gave

For You have redeemed, O Lord, You have redeemed, O Lord
have redeemed us, O Lord, from the grave.

Glory to You, O Father, Glory to You, O Son
Glory to You, O Spirit, Who saves.
Amen.

Versicle

The apple of Your eye
keep us

Under Your wing's shadow
protect us.

Kyrie/Our Father

Lord, have mercy; Christ, have mercy; Lord, have mercy

Our Father, Who art in Heaven,
hallowed be Thy name;
Thy kingdom come,
Thy will be done
on earth as it is in Heaven.
Give us this day our daily bread,
and forgive us our trespasses,
as we forgive those who trespass against us;
and lead us not into temptation,
but deliver us from evil.
Amen.

Nunc Dimittis

Antiphon
Lord now protect our waking
watch over us in sleeping
with Christ our watch be keeping
in peace our rest be taking.

Lord now, You let me go
in peace with word fulfilled

Salvation You did show
in sight of every eye

And You the nations know
revealed, in glory's light

Of Israel's below
the Trinity's on high.
Amen.

Repeat Antiphon

Collect

Visit, we beseech Thee, Lord
this house in which we dwell

Let Angels who abide herein
the devil's snares dispel

In peace, please keep our weary heads
and Thy blessings always as well.

Through Christ Our Lord.
Amen.

Final Blessing

May the almighty and merciful Trinity
bless and protect us for eternity.
Amen.

Marian Antiphons

Alma Redemptoris Mater
Sung from Advent until the Purification

Holy Mother of our Redeemer
Heaven's Gate and Star of the Sea
though we fall, we rise with all nature
and with Gabriel, wonder at thee
who gave birth to thy Son and Creator
Ever-Virgin, take pity on me.

Ave Regina Caelorum

Sung from the Purification until Maundy Thursday

Hail Empress of Angels and Heaven
hail our root and portal of light
rejoice ye of glory resplendent
and plead Christ may pity our plight.

Regina Caeli

Sung from Holy Saturday until Trinity Sunday

Alleluia! Queen, be joyful!
Alleluia! The Son thou bore
Alleluia! Did what He promised
He rises to die no more!
To His Father, our prayers, implore!
Alleluia! Alleluia!

Salve Regina
Sung from Trinity Sunday until Advent

Our Queen and our hope
toward thee we grope
in this valley of exile and tears
turn merciful eyes
O Advocate wise
on us, 'til thy fruit, Christ, appears.

About the Author

B.G. 'Odo' Bonner, Obl. O.S.B., is an Oblate at Clear Creek Abbey in Oklahoma, and took his oblate name after St. Odo of Cluny. He and his wife have been married for over two decades, and have five children. He converted to Catholicism during Protestant seminary, and beyond writing poetry, also teaches and speaks on philosophy, theology, and literature. He was born on the feast of St. Blaise, patron of throats, and has not stopped talking ever since.

About the Illustrator

Gwyneth Thompson-Briggs is a contemporary sacred artist in the perennial Western tradition. Her art decorates churches, schools, and private homes throughout the Americas and Europe. She lives in St. Louis with her husband and four children.